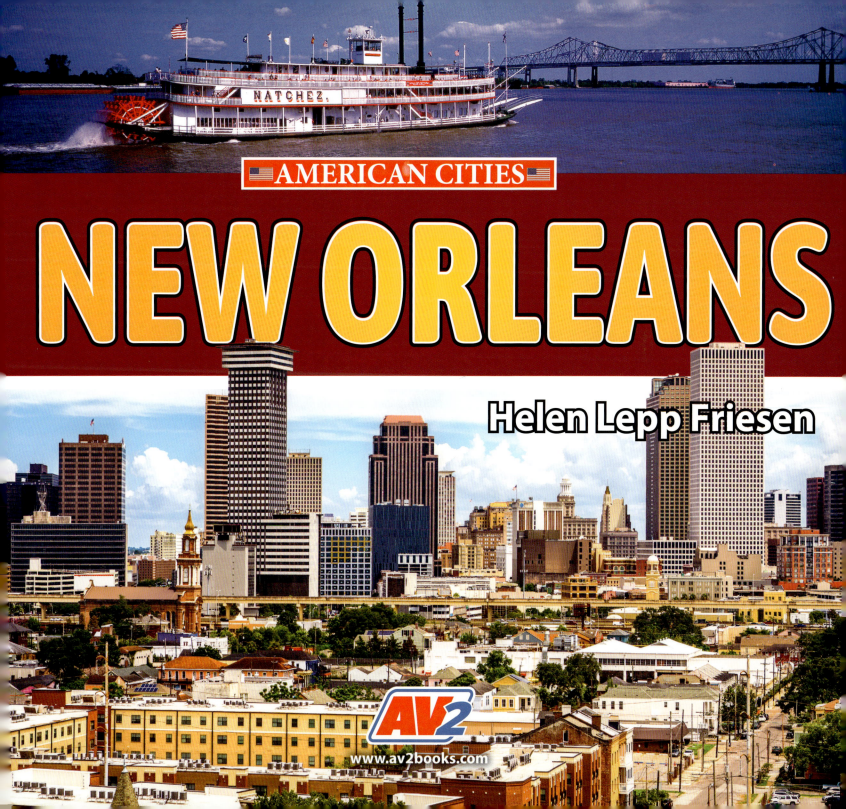

AMERICAN CITIES

NEW ORLEANS

Helen Lepp Friesen

AV2
www.av2books.com

Step 1
Go to www.av2books.com

Step 2
Enter this unique code

WYKBD6IW4

Step 3
Explore your interactive eBook!

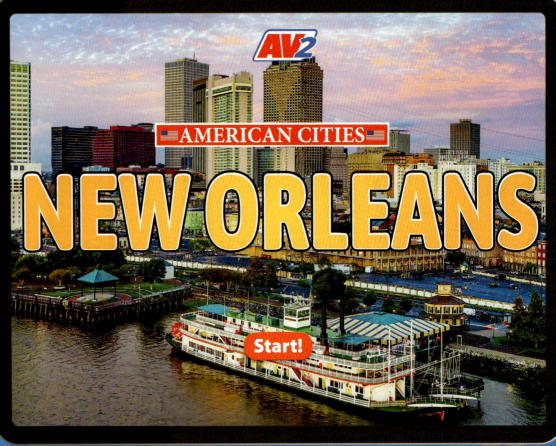

AMERICAN CITIES

NEW ORLEANS

Start!

Your interactive eBook comes with...

AV2 is optimized for use on any device

Audio
Listen to the entire book read aloud

Videos
Watch informative video clips

Weblinks
Gain additional information for research

Try This!
Complete activities and hands-on experiments

Key Words
Study vocabulary, and complete a matching word activity

Quizzes
Test your knowledge

Slideshows
View images and captions

View new titles and product videos at www.av2books.com

Contents

2   AV2 Book Code
4   Get to Know New Orleans
6   Where Is New Orleans?
8   Climate
10 Population and Geography
12 Many Peoples
14 Tourism
16 Sports
18 Economy
20 New Orleans Timeline
22 Things to Do in New Orleans
24 Key Words

Get to Know New Orleans

New Orleans is the largest city in the state of Louisiana. It is known as the birthplace of jazz music. New Orleans is sometimes called "The Big Easy." This is because of its relaxed, easy pace.

Map of Louisiana

ARKANSAS

LOUISIANA

TEXAS

MISSISSIPPI

DeQuincy Railroad Museum, DeQuincy

Cypress Island Preserve

● **BATON ROUGE**

Laura Plantation, Vacherie

Lake Pontchartrain

★ **NEW ORLEANS**

Gulf of Mexico

United States Map

Alaska   Hawaii   Louisiana

MAP LEGEND

★ New Orleans
● Capital City

▮ Louisiana
▮ United States

SCALE 0 — 60 Miles   N

Where Is New Orleans?

New Orleans is on the southern tip of Louisiana. It is 81 miles southeast of Baton Rouge, Louisiana's capital city. You can get there from New Orleans by driving on the I-10 highway.

There are many other exciting places to visit in Louisiana. You can use a road map to plan a trip. Which roads could you take from New Orleans to get to these other places? How long might it take you to get to each place?

TRAVELING LOUISIANA
New Orleans to Lake Pontchartrain 21 miles
New Orleans to Vacherie 52 miles
New Orleans to Cypress Island Preserve 135 miles
New Orleans to DeQuincy 229 miles

Climate

New Orleans has a mild climate. Summers are warm, with a few hot days. Winters are cool, but not cold. New Orleans is a rainy city. Rain can fall at any time of year.

Large storms called hurricanes sometimes pass through the city. These storms bring heavy rain with them. They often cause floods.

More than **60 inches** of rain falls on New Orleans every year. That is almost **twice** the U.S. average.

Population and Geography

New Orleans is home to about 391,000 people. Another 1.2 million people live in the area around the city. The population of New Orleans is slowly growing. Many people moved away in 2005. This was when Hurricane Katrina hit the city.

New Orleans was built on the banks of the Mississippi River. This river is more than 2,200 miles long. It is the second-longest river in the country. Only the Missouri River is longer.

Many Peoples

Aboriginal Peoples lived in the New Orleans area long before anyone else. The French explored the area in the 1600s. They claimed it for France. Settlers began to arrive over time. The French founded the city of New Orleans in 1718.

The Spanish took over Louisiana, and New Orleans, in 1763. Both were returned to France in 1800. France sold Louisiana to the United States three years later.

In **1721**, only **470 people** lived in New Orleans.

Tourism

Most visitors to New Orleans take time to see the French Quarter. This is the oldest part of the city. The French Quarter is known for its old buildings, colorful gardens, and vibrant street life.

The city's Mardi Gras festival is the largest in the country. It lasts for about two weeks. Parades are held every day. There are also several dance parties.

New Orleans welcomes about **1.4 million** visitors every year during **Mardi Gras**.

Sports

New Orleans has two main sports teams. The Pelicans play basketball for the city. They use Smoothie King Center for their home games.

The Saints are the city's main football team. They play their home games at the Mercedes-Benz Superdome. New Orleans hosts the Sugar Bowl every year. It is one of the oldest college football bowl games in the country.

Economy

Tourism is important to New Orleans. In 2018 alone, more than 18.5 million people visited the city. These people spent money on hotels and food.

New Orleans is a port city. Goods are shipped to and from the city every day. New Orleans is one of the world's most important grain ports. Oil is also shipped from the city.

Tourism brings New Orleans about **$9 billion** per year.

New Orleans Timeline

4,300 years ago
Aboriginal Peoples live on the land that is now New Orleans.

1682
René-Robert Cavelier, Sieur de La Salle, claims the area for France.

1718
The city of New Orleans is founded.

1763
Spain takes control of New Orleans.

1788 The Great Fires of New Orleans take place. Many French buildings are lost.

1803 Louisiana, and New Orleans, are sold to the United States.

2005 Hurricane Katrina hits New Orleans, killing about 1,100 people.

2018 LaToya Cantrell becomes New Orleans' first female mayor.

Things to Do in New Orleans

Steamboat *Natchez*
This steamboat takes people on a trip along the Mississippi River. Guests can listen to jazz music as they cruise past several New Orleans landmarks.

Audubon Aquarium of the Americas
About 15,000 sea creatures live at this aquarium. Visitors can pet a shark and view a rare white alligator.

Mardi Gras World
More than three-quarters of all the city's Mardi Gras floats are made here. Visitors can tour the site to see how these floats are made.

Louis Armstrong Park
This park was built to honor jazz musician Louis Armstrong. He was born in the city. The park is often used to host concerts and music festivals.

Louisiana Children's Museum
Covering 8.5 acres, this museum features a bubble studio, a kid-sized kitchen, and a model of the Mississippi River.

KEY WORDS

Research has shown that as much as 65 percent of all written material published in English is made up of 300 words. These 300 words cannot be taught using pictures or learned by sounding them out. They must be recognized by sight. This book contains 110 common sight words to help young readers improve their reading fluency and comprehension. This book also teaches young readers several important content words, such as proper nouns. These words are paired with pictures to aid in learning and improve understanding.

Page	Sight Words First Appearance
4	get, know, to
5	as, because, big, city, in, is, it, its, new, of, sometimes, state, the, this
7	a, are, by, can, could, each, from, how, long, many, might, miles, on, other, places, take, there, these, use, where, which, you
8	almost, any, at, but, days, every, few, has, large, more, not, often, than, that, them, they, through, time, with, year
11	about, and, another, around, away, country, home, live, moved, only, people, river, was, when
12	before, began, both, for, later, over, three, took, were
15	also, lasts, life, most, old, part, see, two
16	one, play, their
19	food, goods, important, world
20	land, now
21	first, great
22	along, do, sea, things, white
23	all, he, here, made

Page	Content Words First Appearance
4	New Orleans
5	The Big Easy, birthplace, Louisiana, music, pace
7	Baton Rouge, highway, map, roads, tip, trip
8	average, climate, floods, hurricanes, inches, rain, storms, summers, winters
11	area, banks, geography, Hurricane Katrina, Mississippi River, Missouri River, population
12	Aboriginal Peoples, France, French, settlers, Spanish, United States
15	buildings, festival, French Quarter, gardens, Mardi Gras, parades, parties, tourism, visitors, weeks
16	basketball, games, Mercedes-Benz Superdome, Pelicans, Saints, Smoothie King Center, sports, Sugar Bowl, teams
19	economy, hotels, money, oil, ports
20	control, René-Robert Cavelier, Spain, timeline
21	fires, LaToya Cantrell, mayor
22	alligator, Audubon Aquarium of the Americas, guests, landmarks, creatures, shark, Steamboat *Natchez*
23	acres, concerts, floats, kitchen, Louis Armstrong Park, Louisiana Children's Museum, Mardi Gras World, model, musician, site, studio

Published by AV2
350 5th Avenue, 59th Floor   New York, NY 10118
Website: www.av2books.com

Copyright ©2021 AV2
All rights reserved. No part of this publication may be reproduced, stored in a retrieval system, or transmitted in any form or by any means, electronic, mechanical, photocopying, recording, or otherwise, without the prior written permission of the publisher.

Library of Congress Cataloging-in-Publication Data
Names: Friesen, Helen Lepp, 1961- author.
Title: New Orleans / Helen Lepp Friesen.
Description: New York, NY : AV2 by Weigl, [2021] | Series: American cities | Audience: Ages 6-9 | Audience: Grades 2-3 | Summary: "American Cities takes young readers on a tour of our capitals and major centers. Each book explores the geography, history, and people that give the featured city its distinctive flair."-- Provided by publisher.

Identifiers: LCCN 2019039071 (print) | LCCN 2019039072 (ebook) | ISBN 9781791115906 (library binding) | ISBN 9781791115913 (paperback) | ISBN 9781791115920 | ISBN 9781791115937
Subjects: LCSH: New Orleans (La.)--Description and travel--Juvenile literature.
Classification: LCC F379.N5 F76 2021 (print) | LCC F379.N5 (ebook) | DDC 917.63/3504--dc23
LC record available at https://lccn.loc.gov/2019039071
LC ebook record available at https://lccn.loc.gov/2019039072

Printed in Guangzhou, China
1 2 3 4 5 6 7 8 9 0   24 23 22 21 20

012020
100919

Project Coordinator: Heather Kissock   Designer: Ana María Vidal

AV2 acknowledges Getty Images, Alamy, Newscom, and Shutterstock as the primary image suppliers for this title.